Little Business Book: Insider Guide To Starting A Passionate Business From Scratch

Arabelle Yee

ISBN-13: 978-1519567949
ISBN-10: 1519567944
For print or media interviews with Arabelle, please contact
teamarabelle@thecalmedge.com

www.arabelleyee.com

DEDICATION

This book is dedicated to you.

CONTENTS

Introduction

I wrote this book out of frustration. I see so many gifted people who are ready to make an impact in the world. They're passionate about what they do and they are ready to share their gift with the world. They want to build a business that's aligned to their purpose and life's calling so they can use it as vehicle to make a change in the world. However, they don't know what to do when it comes to the *business side of things*.

They dabble. They try this and that. It doesn't work and they give up.

If you're reading this book, I know you're one of them; heart-centered and conscious business owners who want to make a difference in the world with what you do.

I wrote this book to help you get started without having to spend months or years dabbling in your business. I wrote this book so you can learn from all the mistakes I made, everything I learned from my journey and my mentors, collapse the timelines and get started on your journey as fast as possible.

I'm originally from Burma and I've been an entrepreneur since the age of 8. I saw my opportunity to sell frozen juice bars to the builders who were working day and night. I sold, they bought and the business started!

Business is something that excites me and I have the passion for it. Having had two businesses while working full-time in the corporate job, I always knew that one day I'd quit my full-time job for good. If you're at the stage where you're thinking of doing the same, I understand that it's very scary but it can be very rewarding if you plan well. I was so secure in my 6-figure income job that to think about starting something from scratch was indeed very scary. However, it was a series of reminders that life showed me put me on my path.

After going through *four* major accidents in my life with the last being diagnosed with Anxiety Disorder, I started to question myself *"What am I doing here? Why am I even worried about things that don't really matter? What's my purpose?"*. I was going through the motions of life, what I was taught growing up and by the society – get as many degrees as you can, get a well paid job, be successful, get married and settle down. I did almost all of that. I got two bachelor degrees and a master's degree. I got myself a well paying 6-figure income job. I got married. I had almost everything I wanted.

But…what was missing? Meaning.

At the end of the day, everyone wants to know if they mattered, if they've given abundantly, loved wholeheartedly and lived fully. That was when I decided to leave my *so-called successes* and started everything from scratch; a business that has meaning and that I can use as a vehicle to make a difference.

Every business evolves. The more you allow your business to evolve rather than holding onto the idea of how it should be, the faster your business will grow.

I'm a certified Clinical Psychotherapist and a NLP Practitioner. That was how I started my business. It was easier to get into the market for me but I always knew what I wanted to do; create deep emotional and spiritual transformations for the people I work with. It was a great journey and learning curve for me.

Then I grew out of it. I realised it when people were coming to me for business advices and I felt called to do that. So I acted on it. In business it's about strategic implementation, with speed. This is where it's also important to know your *why*. Because I always know my *why*, I never derailed from what I want to achieve – create deep inner transformations so people can get connected with who they are and bring out their gifts and message into the world. So I've evolved into a Business Coach who helps clients with their mindset and create transformations. And today, I've worked with clients from across the globe helping them break through their psychological barriers and build their businesses. I'm featured on several major online publications. I've been speaking on stages from mindset, business to transformations.

My journey doesn't end here. I'll continue to grow and I'm already planning my next evolution. This time it'll be less about business but more about connecting to humanity, becoming conscious beings and creating that ripple affect that starts with one small act.

For now, everything I've shared in this book is from the strategies I've learned, implemented and what I think would be most suitable to you while you're starting out. One thing I want to highlight is that I didn't build my business based on strategies alone. In fact, in business mindset plays a big role. I believe in marrying business with spirituality and mindset because when you do that, you grow, your business grows, your finances grow and your clients grow.

What more could you ask for?

Enjoy,

Arabelle Yee

$ Chapter 1

Set Your Foundation

Gone are the days where we plan to work until we reach the age of 60 so that we can retire and enjoy life. We're in the *new age* where we're doing things the new way. What's the new way?

There are more and more solopreneurs venturing out into the entrepreneurial world leaving their 9-5 jobs. There are now more freelancers working on their business part-time so once they're ready, they can get out of the 9-5 grind.

Building a business has never been easier because now is the time where you have access to all the support, courses, coaches, programs and materials at your fingertips such as this book.

When you're starting a business, it's very common for people to jump straight into thinking about sales and marketing. It's understandable because business is directly related to profits and revenues.

However, if you don't have your foundations in place solidly, you'll realise very soon that you're going without a direction, not knowing what your end goal is, not having the step-by-step strategy, pricing your products or services wrong and eventually not meeting your target income goals or not being able to create the lifestyle that you want. Sure I believe in making mistakes so you can learn from them. I've made lots of them but that's the whole reason why I'm writing this book – so you don't have to make the same mistakes but create shortcuts to where you want to be as soon as possible.

That's the aim of this book so you know exactly where you're going and what you have to do next.

Many people get themselves out of their corporate 9-5 job and get into their businesses, only to find out they're working harder than ever and having to sacrifice many things in their life. That's also where many people quit being a business owner because they believe 'it's not for them'.

It's not true.

Yes you need to work hard, put all your time and effort in at the start but if you have the right strategy, systems and processes in place, you can have the ideal lifestyle that you want – whether traveling around with your partner, family or buying your dream house. I'm not saying it'll happen over night. Mastery takes commitment and time. This isn't a quick fix or get rich quick book. It doesn't happen anyway.

But what if you can do what you love and have fun building your business? Many people think I don't have a business because I'm having too much fun. I did have my down days at the start. I had my first ever panic attack in my life when I was starting out. I thought I was going to fail. However, it's a trial and error and like I said, I made lots of errors.

So what if you can do what you love and have fun building your business with very little mistake? It would be cool right? Now, let's move onto the first topic.

Lifestyle

Now, this is important because this is how you're going to live your life. Your business is an extension of you. Your business is a vehicle to help you achieve your dreams, goals and desires.

In order for you to steer your business into a direction that can support the ideal lifestyle that you want, you first need to know what kind of lifestyle you want to have.

You might want a nice house by the beach, a nice car, may be a yacht or you might want to own a big healing centre where people come all the way from all over the world for them to have spiritual, mental, emotional and physical healings. Either way, you might also be thinking *may be only in 5-10 years' time.*

What if it can happen earlier than that?

This is how the brain works; if you believe what you

want is in the future, it'll always be in the future. To condition your brain that it's possible for you and that the future you want is not as far as you think, you need to think of it as *it's happening now.*

So imagine you're living the ideal lifestyle you want *now.* I want you to write down answers to the following questions as specifically as possible –

- What would it look like?

- What does it involve?

- What do you own?

- What would you be doing?

- How much money do you have in cash?

- How much debt do you have?

- How satisfied are you with your life?

- How much money would you need to make to maintain that lifestyle?

Mindset

Tony Robbins says in business 80% is mindset and 20% is mechanics. This is true. I've had the first hand experience and I always say that business is one of the best personal development tools ever. In fact, it's a daily spiritual, emotional and financial practice where you get to learn and grow.

That's, if you allow yourself to go to areas that you
don't want to go – such as your fears, self-esteem and
deep-seated underlying emotional blocks that are
holding you back in life.

After working with many of my private coaching
clients from across the globe, I realise that it doesn't
matter where we're from, we all have the same
challenges. And that's the emotional baggage that we
bring from years of experience.

"It's impossible", said Pride.

"It's risky", said Experience.

"It's pointless", said Reason.

"Give it a try", whispered the Heart.

"You're worth it", said the Soul.

There are many personal glass ceilings that are
holding us back in life and business that we don't
even know. I know this because I've been working on
myself for years spiritually, emotionally and
financially. This is gong to be my lifelong work. Since
very early on, I realise that in order for me to achieve
success (whatever your definition of success is) and to
achieve results, I need to work inside out.

Your business is the extension of yourself. I can give you all the strategies and step-by-step approach but if you don't work inside out, at one point, your growth will be stunted.

I've done many personal development, spiritual and emotional development in my life. I'm still uncovering, working through and breaking through many barriers. It's not an overnight job.

It takes time, awareness and consistency.

Just like you have to brush your teeth every day, just like you have to eat every day, you also have to work on yourself everyday.

This is what one of my clients said after working with her. *"Thanks so much. So last night, with your wise words in mind, I followed through with what I know is the right decision, once and for all. Really scared, but had to be done for emotional wellbeing. I found that strength!"*

Please bear in mind that this isn't a complete exercise where you'll find yourself straightaway but this is a good start to uncover a bit about yourself.

- What are you good at?

- What are you not good at?

- What are the negative things you're telling

yourself? ("I'm not good enough" "I'm bad at_____")

- How would your life transform if you don't have those thoughts about yourself?

- What keeps you awake at night?

- How likely are those worries to turn into reality?

- What are you afraid of?

- What would you do if you weren't afraid?

Finding Your Passion

Many times we hear people say how successful they are, what business they're doing and how much money they're making.

And many times, we fall into the trap of comparing ourselves and our lives with those of others. So when someone comes along and tells us *this is what you should be doing*, we quickly turn that idea into a business we don't even know if we're passionate about.

Sidenote: Passion isn't just about doing what we love. Passion is about doing what we love, being ready to face whatever consequence it comes with it and willing to do whatever it takes to achieve it.

So what are you passionate about? Let's do a quick exercise.

- What were you like when you were a child?

- What was one thing that you always enjoyed doing?

- When did you lose that passion?

- What did you think you'd become when you were young?

- How is your adult life different from what you've always wanted to do?

Growing up, we meet people, we make new friends, we pick up hobbies and we listen to what other people think. Slowly we change, evolve and turn into someone else. Along the way, we lose what we're innately good at and we start to live our life according to the social norm.

We go to school and university taking up majors that will get us *the right job that pays well*. While we gained the certifications and status, we slowly lose ourselves.

Running a business isn't a job. It's a lifestyle because we're going to spend majority of our waking and also sleeping time working on it. Being an entrepreneur or a business owner is a lifestyle.

It might as well be something we're passionate about.
Don't you think?

Money Block

Now here's my favourite topic: Money. Let me ask
you this first – what comes to your mind when you
think about money?

Money is only a reflection of our beliefs. Money is
only a tool that helps us achieve our dreams and
desires. Money is only a symbol.

When couples argue about money, when you're
struggling financially and when you feel *icky* when you
think about money, it's not about money.

There, I said it.

It's about your beliefs, psychological limitations and
your ability to make an impact. Many people say –

*"When I have a million dollars, I want to start my own
charity"*

"Money breaks marriages"

"Money is evil"

"Money makes people arrogant"

"Money is so hard to make"

"I have to work really hard and sacrifice a lot of things if I

want to make lots of money"

"Money is status"

Do you resonate with any of that? So again, you could have the best strategies to build a life and business you want but if you have your own personal glass ceilings about money, it's going to be so hard for you.

Let me give you a few real life examples of people who struggled with money blocks, how the blocks held them back in life and the breakthroughs they get after realising, acknowledging and working through them.

Example 1

One of my clients has a big vision about her business and her future. She's also extremely hard working and she executed every strategy I gave her in her business, however, she just couldn't make money in her business. After working through her mindset barriers, we found out a deep-seated problem. She grew up in a very rich family and all her life, she never had to worry about money.

Her parents and grandparents had always supported her financially so among her friends, she was seen as this rich kid who got everything she wanted without having to put any effort or use her abilities. So since young, she told herself *subconsciously* that she had no ability to do whatsoever and that she could never make money without the support from her parents and grandparents.

As a result, she'd do everything to sabotage every opportunity that came up for her to make money. After working on her mindset, confidence and self-esteem, she's now not only charging what she's worth, she's exceeding her target income goals.

Example 2

This client of mine has always been good at making lots of money in her life, until she got married. She's a risk taker, she thrives on challenges and she's good at making money. However, her partner is the opposite of her: cautious, plays safe and sceptical about everything. So when she started her business, she was repeatedly told that she was aiming too high and that she would never make the money she wanted because life isn't fair and it's not that easy.

Coming from someone she trusts and loves repeatedly, over time she really started to take on all his projection of his own limitations and applied on herself. As a result, every time she has a chance to get a new client, she sabotaged herself and subconsciously communicated her own limitations, worries and low self-esteem to her potential clients.

It took a while for me to work this through with her. Once she got a breakthrough, she's now able to create

$5-8k clients in just one conversation.

These money blocks are like parasites. They are there working behind the scenes eating away your confidence, self-worth and self-love. They are hidden away in the dark corners of your mind. They're in stealth mode so that you don't even know you have them.

Here's the last example of my own money block.

Example 3

I grew up around so many rich families and most of my friends were rich kids. When I say rich, I'm talking about millions of dollars in cash rich. However, there's an ugly side of it. The rich husbands were too rich, they didn't have anything else to do, they started cheating on their wives. The wives, while knowing what their husbands were to up to, they believed they had an image to maintain. So instead, they surrounded themselves with luxury, status and wrong people creating that image of a perfect life.

As a result, kids were all over the place – most of whom were my friends. So growing up, I *subconsciously* decided that money makes people evil, especially men. So I decided that I needed to work my butt off to out-earn the man I'm in a relationship with so that I can be safe. That caused a lot of tensions in my past relationships because I was always measuring the success of a relationship with how much I can make more than them, making the men in my life feel they weren't as good as me. My ego took over. When ego gets involved, things never turn out nice.

I've been working on my own money blocks and I've seen massive transformations not only in my business but also in my personal life. After all, whatever goes on in my personal life affects my business as well.

So let's talk about your money blocks. I say *your* money blocks because I know you have them. You just don't know where they are yet. Money blocks something that come up in every stage of our financial growth. So let's do this.

- What did you learn about money growing up?

- What were you taught about money?

- Write down 5-10 words when you think about the word 'money'.

- What is the financial situation of people around you? (Jim Rohn said 'You're the average of 5 people around you'. Who you surround yourself with tell a lot about where you're in life)

- What's your biggest struggle when it comes to

making money?

- What are your beliefs about money?

- How capable are you to make the money that you want?

- How much money are you saving every month?

- What negative beliefs about money can you let go of today?

When you're ready to break through your money blocks, I've created a free audio to help you identify and remove them. You can click here to listen.

Gratitude

Gratitude is such an underrated word. We humans are very good at complaining or focusing on what we don't have rather than what we have.

The other day, I was talking to a client of mine and he said, "Facebook is so ridiculous. They just want to make money and charge us for the advertising". I was thinking, aren't we lucky that we have Facebook? Facebook has connected people from all over the world. Facebook has helped thousands of businesses succeed and generate millions of dollars just from Facebook advertising alone. Compared to other social medias, Facebook is by far the most effective platform for majority of businesses.

This is just one example. What are you complaining about in your life? Are you focusing on things you don't have rather than what you have? Are you focusing on how much money you don't have, while totally ignoring your bank balance or the people around you who will be there to support you no matter what?

While you're able to sit in a café and drink a cappuccino, there are many people going bankrupt, getting hungry or losing their houses. Now, I'm not saying that you should be guilty or be content with that $200 you have in your bank but what I'm saying is *it's the little things that count.*

"Where your focus goes, your energy flows – Tony Robbins"

Let's talk about the energy and universe.

You don't have to be a fan of the Law of Attraction. It's cool. But I want to tell you a little bit about this so you understand the power of gratitude. This also isn't some airy-fairy concept. This is science. Trust me, I'm all about marrying science and spirituality.

The Law of Attraction is about Law of Vibration. We're vibrating human beings meaning we're energy beings. We can't see the wind or electricity but we know they are there and they are energy. Likewise, the energy we have in our body is something we can't see but we can feel it. That's why we say things like "I don't have energy today". Just the energy alone in our brain is enough to power a light bulb. I wish I could plug a power cable in my head and show you. I'm saying this from research and science.

So how is this related to gratitude? Well, when we're in a certain mental and emotional state, our energy vibrates in different frequencies. We're like walking WI-FI stations. Whatever frequency we emit, we attract similar frequencies.

So when we're grateful for the things we have in our life, rather than what we don't have, we vibrate in a frequency that we call *positivity*. That's how the universe works. When we're flowing with positive energy, then our energy antenna will tune into other positive energies out there in the universe.

To be honest, it's not about *attracting* what you want. I believe that you can't really attract what you're not. You can only attract what you're. That means, when we're grateful for the things that we have, the universe sees you as the big plus sign walking around and it wants to give you more pluses in your life.

Also when we're grateful, it changes the chemicals in our body, which lifts our mood and make us happy. When we start making it a habit, then we're more

likely to focus on positive opportunities rather than
the negative ones.

So what are you grateful for?

List down the things you have today. (From $200 in
your bank account, the $2.5 left on your gift
vouchers, car, house, your abilities, talent,
certifications, your story, your message, etc.)

Create a 7-day challenge for yourself to write down 1
thing a day that you're grateful for. (When I did this
last time, I wrote down "I'm grateful that I still have
toothpaste to brush my teeth")

Pick 5 things that you're grateful for and start
focusing more on it because where you focus goes
your energy flows.

Your Vision & Mission

Setting a vision and mission isn't only for corporate
companies. It's for small businesses, solopreneurs and
for your own personal life as well. Visions are your
dreams; what you'd like to achieve on a bigger scale.
Whereas your mission is what you need to do to
achieve that vision.

When starting your business, it's important to have a
vision and a mission that's aligned to your life's calling
and purpose. It should give you enough reason to go
through all the challenges that come with running a

business.

> *"If your dreams don't scare you, they aren't big enough - Ellen Johnson Sirleaf"*

Your vision is based on your 'why', it'll steer you back to the right direction when you derail. Here's my vision.

My vision is to inspire and empower people so they can break through their personal glass ceilings, access their inner strength and make a massive impact in the world. My vision is to see the world filled with conscious people supporting, helping and loving each other so the world becomes a safe place for all beings to live in.

My mission is to support that through my business, by educating and creating transformations in people's lives and businesses so they can start that ripple effect in the world.

Does it sound big? Yes it does. Does it scare me? Hell, it does. Is it possible? It's a resounding yes.

So what is your vision and mission? How will you make that happen through your business?

My vision is

_____

_____

_____

_____

_____

_____

_____

My mission is

_____

_____

_____

_____

_____

_____

_____

Strategy

A business without a strategy is like a ship without a rudder. You're going everywhere, which means you're not getting anywhere. However, for you to know your strategy, you need start with an outcome first.

You've set your vision and mission. You now know what you'd like to achieve in the long term. How long? 5 years? 10 years?

"Every business needs to start with an end goal in mind" – Arabelle Yee

Every business needs to start with an end goal in

mind. Are you selling your business in five years' time? Are you going to turn into an organisation with hundreds of employees? Are you going to branch out? Are you going global?

Once you know your end goal, you need to break it down in smaller chunks so it becomes executable. Start with a 12 months roadmap. Then break it down into quarterly, monthly, weekly and daily. Yes, you need to be that specific so you can benchmark how much you've achieved and if you've met your target goals.

You also need to know your numbers. Business is about numbers, whether you want to deal with that part or not. The success of your business depends on how much income you generate. We'll talk more about numbers, budgeting and managing your Finances in the Chapter 4.

For now, let's start with the high-level strategy.

- What's your end goal for your business?

- How much money do you want to make in a year?

- What does that mean in terms of monthly, weekly and daily income?

12-months Roadmap

What do you want to achieve in 12 months time?			
	Q1 Goals	Q2 Goals	Q3 Goals	Q4 Goals
Tasks				
Income				
Clients				
Lifestyle				
Others				

$ Chapter 2

Now, we're getting into the nitty gritty details of starting a business. These are the steps people skip. When starting a business, many feel that they need to create a website and Facebook first, which is far from true.

What are you going to write on your website? How will people know what you're offering is for them?

Think about it like this. Business is like a dating game, although I haven't done that for a while now, but I still remember the rules!

When you're looking for a partner, do you say I'll take anyone who comes my way? No! Right? You have a checklist of criteria. That's why people say, "He ticks all the boxes". It's a mental checklist of what you're looking for in your partner.

It's something like:

- Kind, caring and open-minded

- Able to stand on his own feet

- Confident, charming and sociable enough to fit in with my friends

- Tall and strong but don't need to be handsome

- Grounded and Spiritual (a double bonus!)

- Can hold a good conversation and intellectual

- Have a great chemistry

- Someone who I can feel safe with

- Fun, adventurous and likes outdoors

- Likes dogs and can laugh at my lame jokes

Wow! I just got my own list. Ok, moving on.

So now you know what kind of a man you're looking for, you also need to know if they're looking for a person like you. So for them to know you're someone they're looking for, you need to put yourself out there and share your story.

You might need to go to places they hang out. You might need to sign up on dating websites (only paid and legitimate ones please!). And when you finally meet the person, you need to tell them a bit about yourself too so that both of you'ren't wasting your time and both of you can find out if you share the same values and perspective towards life. This is where sharing your story comes in.

Share Your Story

"Your story is the key that unlocks someone

else's prison. Share you testimony."

In business, sharing your story is such a powerful tool because it shows people who the person behind that brand or logo is, and that you're just like them. You have to be brave enough to be vulnerable and share both your challenges and successes. That way people will know how far you've come, what you've gone through and what you've experienced. Of course, you need to use common sense to know what to share. At the end of the day, people are only interested in one thing; about themselves. They want to know if you have the same values (this is subconscious decision), if you know what you're talking about, if you're someone they can relate to and they can trust.

So here's my story.

I was originally from Burma where the country was closed from the rest of the world for decades. I grew up spending a lot of time exploring, spending time in nature and with animals. We used to live in a little wooden house but in our neighbourhood, we were rich so I spent days helping my neighbours, people living in huts, in their little makeshift shops selling betel nut, vegetables, helped milk the cows and carry water from the communal well that almost the whole neighbourhood used. I've always had a passion to help people.

However, there's another side of my life; living

among the rich society. Society has taught me that when I grew up, I had to get a good degree, find a good job and have status. So I did all of that. I got two Bachelor degrees, a Masters degrees and uncountable certificates. Very early on in my corporate career, I started making 6-figure salary and to me status was everything – until I had a wake-up call.

I went through a series of major accidents, four to be exact, from getting both bones in my leg broken, being in a major car accident where my car was crushed under a massive military truck, getting admitted to hospital with internal bleeding to the last one getting diagnosed with Anxiety Disorder. When I was lying on the hospital bed after getting diagnosed with Anxiety Disorder, I started to question everything in my life.

I also realised that life was giving me a blaring alarm that I wasn't living my purpose and things weren't on the right track but I kept snoozing it until I couldn't anymore.

I started to ask questions like "What's my purpose? What am I doing here? Did I live fully? Did I love whole-heartedly? Did I give abundantly?"

These are the questions I find many of my clients ask themselves when they come to me. At the end of the day, everyone wanted to know if they mattered.

And you matter.

So that was when I woke up. Woke up to my true self. I realised I want to make a difference and I want to make a big impact in the world and in the lives of people around me. So that's how I started my journey of being a Transformational and Business Coach.

Creating transformations comes natural to me. With all the work I've been doing on myself with personal development, spirituality and mindset, I realised that the more I work on myself, the more I'm able to help others.

And business excites me. I've been an entrepreneur since the age of 8. Coming up with strategies and ideas gets me out of bed every morning with full of energy. Business also enables me to reach more people to create those transformations and start that ripple effect.

So today, I've combined the two and have worked with people, women in general, from across the globe doing exactly just that. I've been speaking on stages sharing my message inspiring and empowering people. I've surrounded myself with spiritual leaders, thought leaders, change makers and conscious business leaders who are making millions of dollars while staying true to themselves. They've in turn helped me expand my brand to reach more people, which means I have the opportunity to help many conscious leaders out there. I've been featured in major online publications being recognised as a thought leader and inspirational leader.

I'm able to do all of this because of only one thing: I allowed myself to step out of fear and be brave enough to live my purpose.

That's what I want for you too.

Now what's your story?

- One thing that I want the most from my business is _____.

- The most rewarding feeling in life is when I do _____.

- The challenges that shaped me to be who I'm today are _____.

- Specific steps I took to overcome those challenges are _____.

- Key milestones that I've achieved in my life are _____.

- What prompted me to start doing what I'm doing is _____.

- 5 points of credibility that will help people build trust in me are _____.

This story that you're sharing is also called your defining moment of story. Those are an event or a string of events that put you on the path where you're now. You'll use this story when you talk to people, on your website, in your talks and on social media.

Your Audience

Now that you know how and why you need to share your story, let's talk about whom you'll specifically share it with.

Let's use the dating example again. So you now have that checklist of what kind of man you're looking for, let's go a little deeper. What's the age range? What type of jobs or businesses does he have? Where does he like to hang out? What's missing in his life that you can complete? You need to know all of this because if you want to meet the right person who you can have fun with while building the life you've always wanted, you need to go to where they are.

"Everyone is not your customer — Seth Godin"

Likewise in business, you need to know exactly who your target audience is. There are a couple of reasons why you need to do this. I know you can help everyone but in reality, you can't. You don't have the budget to market to the whole world. If you market yourself as a generalist in the crowded market place, people won't notice you; at least at the start. This is

the topic that gets people really confused. It's ok for
you to branch out and do many things once you're
successful. You can become a generalist but for a
start, you need to focus on one area and get known
for it. That way, you'll also build *mastery*.

Different people speak different languages. For
example, a 50 year old man who wants to lose weight
might say "I really need to stop drinking beer"
whereas a 30 year old woman who wants to lose
weight will say "I want to gain self-confidence and I
want to start loving myself again". When you market
your services, you need to speak your target
audience's language.

Lastly, if you still do want to market to everyone and
still getting clients, you'll soon realise that you're not
having fun in your business because you're not
working with your ideal clients.

Let me give you an example.

When I was starting out, I really believed I could
work with everyone and I did. I attracted all kinds of
women; those who wanted my services cheap, those
wanted me to do everything for them, those who
want to blame everyone and not take responsibility.
As a result, I started to get really tired and drained.
My business was no longer exciting for me.

Now, I choose who I work with. My clients are

visionary and heart-centred women who want to make an impact in the world. One of my clients is a mother of three, who recently separated from her husband. Things are challenging for her and she could easily just give herself excuse not to work on her business. But her vision is bigger than herself.

She has a restaurant. She also wanted to build a coaching business. At the same time, she wants to create an organisation in Africa where she can educate women on life, business and mindset. She's giving talks to hundreds of people in churches, in youth camps, in prisons and in meet-up groups. This woman is a powerhouse. As a result, I get excited every time I coach her because I know I'm part of something big. I'm helping her so she can go out and help others and start that ripple effect. Now business is exciting! And rewarding!

If you have a product-based business, it's the same thing. I know someone who has a software company and at the very early stage of his business, he worked with everyone because he wanted to have cash coming in.

However, at one point he realised that he was getting so much complaints and problems in the customer service area. He then realised that it was more of the type of customers he was working with rather than his products or services. He quickly took control of the situation. He fired the customer.

Yes sometimes we need to be brave enough to let the client go. It's all about standing on our ground, being firm in our values and making an informed decision.

He made it clear to himself and to his staff that they choose who they work with. They have their Terms & Conditions revised, they set clear expectations with their customers and if that's what they want, they will work with them.

So back to you – who is your target audience?

- Who do you want to work with?

- What are their burning problems?

- What are their hopes and dreams?

- What do they *want?* (It's not need. They don't know what they need. They know what they want.)

- Where can you find them both online and offline?

- Where do they hang out both online and offline?

Your Products

Here comes the part where a lot of people make mistakes. I don't want you to be one of them.

One of my clients came to me and said she has created all these programs and packages but nobody bought them. So the first question that I asked her was "Did you ask your target audience what they wanted?" and she said no. That's the problem.

Please please please never create anything because you think it's cool or because you think it's what people need. When you have an idea about what you can sell or create, the first thing you need to do is to take it to your target audience and ask them if that's what they want.

There are two ways you can do this.

1. You can find out what the burning problem is that your target audience is facing and create a solution for that.

2. Or you can take your idea to your target audience and ask them if they would buy if you package it in a way that they want.

Let me tell you about what happened to a program I created. When I created my first program, I was so excited. I was the cheering for my own program. I couldn't wait to get it out there. I spent *months* working on it. My target income from that launch was at least $50,000. I had everything in place; affiliate marketing, sales funnels and thousands of dollars worth of bonuses.

Then I launched.

Do you know how much I made from that program?

Zero. Zip. Zilch. Nada! Yep!

It was pretty simple. I didn't ask what they wanted. I created *what I wanted*. Nobody needed that program. So the first step is to find out what burning problems you can solve.

Now the next thing is, how are you going to position your product or services? Are you going to be a premium brand where you charge high-end prices? Or are you going to be affordable brand where many people have easy access to you?

Now, before we get into those details, let me work out something for you.

Meeting your income goals

Say your monthly income goal is $5,000 and you're a Kinesiologist. You charge $150 per hour. That means you need see 33 clients to meet that income goal. We're not even including your marketing costs or other expenses here.

$150 x 33 clients = $5,000

What if you start charging $2,500 for the same client but in a 3-month program? That means you need only 2 clients a month to meet your target income goals.

$2,500 x 2 clients = $5,000

Woah! How can I charge that much? Doing what? It's not the industry standard! Nobody's doing that!

First, my love, I want to say that that's your money block right there! Secondly, you can't compare prices like that because it's not the sessions your clients are getting, it's the result that they're getting! They're paying for their dreams, not for the hours. Plus the mistake people make when setting prices is that,

1. They either compare the prices with what other people are charging or

2. They ask the wrong people like their friends and family members who aren't their ideal clients. I also want to highlight that when people say you can't charge that amount, whatever the amount is, they're only projecting their beliefs about money. It's your product and it's about *you* deciding how much it's worth. So let's look at it again; you charge $2,500 per client for 3-months package. It looks like this. Let me make something up.

3-months Program

"I choose not to work hourly because to create the long term results and to achieve your goals, I work with my clients only a 3-months program basis. During those 3 months, you'll get 12 weekly sessions where we'll work with your energy to align and

balance. After each session, I'll give you tasks you can
do it at home so that you don't lose momentum
during the week. If you need to get in touch with me
during the week, I'm available for you to call me
during office hours so it looks something like this –

- 12 x sessions

- Unlimited access during office hours for
support

- 3 x meditation audios

- 5 x tasks to work during the week"

Now if you have a product-based business, let's talk
about a mobile café as an example. How many
coffees can you sell a day? Say you regularly sell 50
coffees a day.

$4.5 x 50 coffees = $220 per day

However, when it comes to product-based business, it
gets a little bit more complicated because you have to
start thinking about stock, capital expenses and other
expenses. So to cover those costs and to meet your
target income goals, there are a couple of things you
can do; packages or programs. Same thing. As a
mobile café, you can do combos and you can do
catering for groups above 'x' number of people and
charge a set price.

Sidenote: That's why it's eser to start a service-based business. It's faster, easier and less risk.

Different price points

Once you've worked out how much to charge your target income goals, here's another thing; creating different price points. If you have just $2,500 program, it can be hard for you to sell because not everyone will be able to afford it. So if you still want to cater to others with a cheaper option, you can create a smaller product at a smaller price point. It looks something like this using a coaching program as an example.

- **Premium**: Bali Retreat for $9,000

- **High**: 1-1 Coaching for $5,000

- **Med**: Group Coaching for $2,000

- **Low**: 1-hour consultation for $275

- **Free**: Complimentary call for 30 mins

Let me give you an example of a friend of mine who owns a chocolate company. Who doesn't like chocolate? Especially when it's raw and vegan! It's called Pana Chocolate. Most of their products are within a range of $10, which is affordable, but they also have a higher range from gift packs to wedding cakes.

Now here's another example. If you've ever been part
of a membership program, you'll notice that most
have different types of memberships, for example,
Basic, Advanced and Gold membership which comes
at different price points with different offerings.

Verify your idea

Now that you have an idea of what you could
potentially offer that will solve the burning problems
of your target audience, you create them.

NO! YOU DON'T!

You need to verify if that's what people want. So you
can do customer surveys to check in with them to
make sure whatever you're creating is on track. You
don't want to spend weeks and months only to find
out what you've created is a flop.

So, over to you.

- How much money do you want to make a
  year?

- What's your monthly income goal?

- What can you create to solve the burning
  problems of your target audience?

- What are your price points?

- How many people are you going to survey/interview to verify your idea?

- How many people are you'lling to give away your products or services so you can get feedback?

$ Chapter 3

Admin & Background Work

Ahh! Here's everyone's least favourite part. The
tedious admin work! I know, I myself slack in this
area too but don't worry because I'm going to tell you
step-by-step what you can do to minimise headache
and maximise your productivity. Don't you just love
this book? I wish I had this book when I was starting
out!

So everything I'm sharing with you in this book is in a
chronological order, meaning you really don't need to
worry about anything until you reach to that chapter.
Trust me I've made so many mistakes. I've failed. My
stuffs have flopped. I've wasted months and
thousands of dollars. You don't need to do all of
those all over again.

That's what this book is for. My years of mistakes and
lessons compacted into this book so you can collapse
the timelines and create results in the shortest time
possible.

Below is a list of things you'll need or need to do
when starting your business.

- Get ABN number (<u>Apply with Australian
  Business Register</u>)

- Register Business Name ([Australia Securities & Investments Commission](#))

- Get insurance – Public liability insurance & professional indemnity insurance

- Business bank account

- Business credit card

- Customer Relationship Management System (www.mailchimp.com)*

- Online payment system (www.paypal.com)

- Offline payment system (EFTPOS machine from your bank)

- Get domain name for your website (www.godaddy.com)

- Build a website (www.wix.com)*

- Appointment scheduling software (www.acuityscheduling.com)*

- First Aid Certificate**

- Police Check**

Disclaimer: I do not work for any of the organisations or take responsibility. This is only a recommendation from my own personal experience and working with many other business owners. You're advised to do your own research before you commit to paying or applying any of these services. Some of the organisations recommended are only applicable for Australia. If you're in a different country, I believe there'll be equivalent of those organisations.

* I may earn commission when you sign up with these resources.

** Depends on your type of profession and services you provide.

Resources

Every business owner needs a support of a team. We've come to a time where creating a team is so easy and simple that I suggest everyone to get a team on an ad-hoc basis. Especially as a solopreneur, it's natural that you'd want to do everything yourself, however, remember the exercise we did earlier on how much money you want to make a year and then we broke it down to daily income?

Let's use the previous example of your target monthly income goal of $5,000. That means you need to make $31.25 per hour. I'm making this very simple completely ignoring tax, expenses or superannuation.

So imagine you've come to a point where you need an Accountant to work through your piles of receipts and tax. If you're not an expert in that area, you're going to spend hours, if not days, working on it whereas if you get an expert it could possibly be a task that gets done in a couple of hours.

You - $31.25 x 2 days = $500

Accountant - $40 x 3 hours = $120

You get the idea. You need an accountant.

So here is a list of people who can help you on a part-time basis in your business.

- Bookkeeper / Accountant (www.elance.com or hire locally)

- Virtual Assistant (www.elance.com) You can hire VAs for as little as $4 per hour online. If you find the right one, they are extremely helpful and can help you with many things like – appointment booking, customer service, appointment bookings, travel bookings, social media management, writing blog posts, formatting documents and what they can help you with are countless)

- Lawyer

  o Terms & Conditions for your products/Services

  o Privacy Policy for your website

- o Terms of Use for your website

- o Customer contract to protect both parties

- Web Developer. The web-hosting service I suggested above is very easy to use. It's drag and drop. You can sign up today and start creating your website. However if you're not a techy person, you can hire web developers but they can be expensive.

- Graphic Designer (www.fiverr.com)

- Copy Writer (www.elance.com). When you create sales pages on your website, copywriters can help you write copies that sell. They can be expensive but if you find the right ones, they can definitely help boost your sales.

$ Chapter 4

Finance, Budgeting & Tax

"Enjoy the moment and plan your money for the future so that you can enjoy every single moment. – Aundria Khine"

Money has become akin to oxygen

Welcome to the chapter talking about Finance. Don't freak out when you hear the word "Finance". Finance is money and money is something we all need to have in order to live in this world. Many of us feel uncomfortable talking about money. If you're one of them, remember the fact that we require money to survive in this world and it has becomes akin to oxygen. Having money is never a bad thing nor talking about it. For me, money is not just about paying off debts, living in a mansion or driving my dream car. Of course I do want all these things in my life too, but it's more about buying my time back. I want to use that time and energy to do more meaningful things in life and give back to the world. When you have more than enough money, you can do more for others, be more successful in your business and fulfil yourself more.

"Successful people make money. It's not that

*people who make money become successful. But
that successful people attract money. They bring
success to what they do - Wayne Dyer"*

Knowing your numbers is a part of your business
process to succeed.

You might say to yourself "I'm not a finance person.
I don't want to deal with all those receipts and bills".
You might hate mathematics but you have to love
counting your money. Ignoring your numbers when
it comes to business is not going to help your
business. The longer you ignore it, the less money
you'll have for yourself and eventually you could have
nothing to show for your hard work. Don't forget
that you're a capable business owner and this is just
another business process that you need to pay
attention to. Let go off all those limiting beliefs of
yourself and start taking action by showing attention
to your money and numbers.

Even if you feel like you're in a financial mess right
now, start where you're at and there is always room to
improve.

So are you ready to take care of your money and bring
more financial abundances into your life?

When your answer is yes -

"No one can make millions and keep millions without learning about personal finance - journeytomillions.com"

TAKE ACTION.

Always start with your personal finance. If you don't take care of your personal finance, you'll never end up taking care of your business finance. You don't have to be an accountant or a financial consultant to take care of your finances. Start with baby steps. None of us learn how to walk and run without crawling and falling over. So don't be scared to make mistakes.

Mistakes allow you to improve your actions the next time. Here are your baby steps to take care of your money

- Doing conscious spending

- Paying your bills on time

- Checking all your statements

- Knowing your debts

- Knowing your numbers

When your baby steps get better (i.e. when you have a brief knowledge about how much money you make and what your expenses are), you can start walking or may be even running. Then, it's time to boost your finance skills by looking into details of your income and expenses.

> *"Your net worth to the world is usually determined by what remains after your bad habits subtracted from your good ones - Benjamin Franklin"*

What do you need to do to look into details?

Record all your income and expenses. Write down everything that you have received and expensed. I have prepared an excel spreadsheet so that if you want to start doing this exercise, this spreadsheet will help you get started.

Why do you need to do it? Because tracking your income and expenses in detail will allow you to have a clear picture of exactly where your money is going. If you're overspending on some expenses, you can take corrective actions straight away before you max out your credit cards or go bankrupt.

This is a simple exercise to monitor your spending habits and to make you become a conscious spender if you allow yourself to become one. If you're doing a good job with your spending, congratulate yourself and say well done. If you see any bad spending habit, thank yourself as you found them and you're going to fix them. Appreciate yourself first and you'll start to appreciate your money.

Let me be clear. Your money mindset and your spending behaviours are going to help you achieve your money goals, not how much money you can make. You can make millions of dollars, but without the right money mindset and good spending habits, you'll never know where your money is going and you'll never have enough money in your bank account. That's why people win lottery but a few months later they're broke again. Look at Hollywood celebrities – they all make good money but why are some so rich and some are so broke? Some go broke because they don't have the right money mindset and they end up sabotaging their income.

When you handle your personal finance well, you won't have problems managing your business finance either. Let's move on to talking about your business finance.

"Financial Management is at the heart of any business. It's one area that can drive it forward."

Separate Bank Accounts

The first step, it's always good to have two separate bank accounts for your personal and business finances. It makes your life easier in the long run.

Having two separate bank accounts will help you
separate your personal and business expenses. You
don't have to manually check them; it saves your
precious time, creates fewer errors, helps you keep
records efficiently and creates less confusion.

*"Be aware of little expenses. A small leak will
sink a great ship. - Benjamin Franklin"*

Creative Spending

Second step - as a start-up business owner, if you
have limited funds to run your business, be careful on
what you invest in. Don't over stock if you're selling
products. If you're required to acquire plant and
equipment for your business, look into both buy and
rent options and go with the cheaper option. You're
going to invest in marketing and advertising to put
yourself out there. Not all social media platforms are
going to work for you so only invest on the platforms
that are bringing clients and customers to your
business. After a few months of testing, you'll know
what social media platforms are working for you so
that you can focus on the ones that are working for
you and stop spending on the ones that don't give
you results.

Renting an office can be expensive. Instead you could
use your spare space at home as your home office. If
you've signed up for programs and memberships, and

if you're paying for recurring fees but not using them, it's time to cancel them. Be creative about your investments and spending in your business. This is going to help you to run your business more efficiently.

Your receipts are money back from ATO

Step three - Keep all your receipts and bills. Put them in a file, write notes on them; why and what you spent it for. That way when the tax season comes, you're all set. You need to keep all your receipts and bills that you have used for tax deductions for 5 years. If you get audited, you have proven records for all your deductions. Stay away from trouble.

Your income is the blood stream to the body of your business.

Forth step - look into details. You've done this with your personal finances so I'm confident that you won't have any problem applying the same method to your business finances. Constantly analyse your business; what products and services are generating the majority of income? What products and services are not? Focus on the products and services that are bringing you income and eliminate the ones that aren't if there's no room for improvement. Do the same checks for your expenses. Avoid expenses that you don't need to spend and keep your cash flowing.

*"It always comes down to the money. The
biggest problem is juggling the cash flow - Dan
Wyman"*

Cash flow

Final Step - manage your cash flow. I left the best for
last. Many small business owners face cash flow
problems and sadly, they have to let go of their
business. Don't let that happen to you. If you plan,
it's less likely that you're going to face it. Selling
products is more risky than selling services.

So how do you plan it? It's a very straightforward
process. Get organised, be in control of your day-to-
day finances and get an accountant to help you with
technical areas.

You need to manage your bad debts. If you're dealing
with cash payments, you're good and safe. But if
you're offering instalment payments or sales/service
on credit term then you need to watch out. Some of
your customers and clients are going to delay paying
your invoices or some may not even bother to pay
unless you work with a debt recovery firm and that's
going to cost you money. Don't be too nice. You
need your money to run your business and take care
of your family. So chase your payment.

If you're just starting out, keep a calendar to follow

up with the payments. If you have a growing business, don't hesitate to have an accounting system, which makes it easier to identify overdue payments. There's no harm in charging a deposit up front and performing credit checks to minimise your risk.

You need to make it flow. If you're selling services it'll be less risky for you. However, if you're selling products and your suppliers are asking you to make payment within 7 to 14 days after delivery then you need to expect payment from your customers before 7 days if you don't have large cash reserves. It's because you can't manage your cash flow. It's going to cause you a big problem with your cash flow if you have to pay your suppliers before you receive payment from your customers. Cash on delivery is the best system to go for dealing with your customers and if you're willing to provide a credit term; the credit term you're providing to your customers has to be shorter than the credit term your suppliers are offering you.

You need to make profit. I know no one that wants to run a business that's making losses. Do you? But how are you going to know that your business is making profit. Start with your pricing. Don't do the same mistake that other smaller business owners do. It's common for a business to be unaware of a total cost of delivering their product or services. Poor pricing can definitely bring down your business. Add all the costs that have incurred producing your final products & services and add your profit margin percentage on top of your total cost. If you feel like it's too hard for you, seek professional advice or check with them to see if you're on the right track.

You need to manage your stock if you're selling products. As a starter, you might want to fill up your store full of stocks, but don't forget that you'll generate cash only when you sell them off. So why would you hold too much stock which might take a while to sell? You don't want to be broke because you used all your cash for stocks and desperately waiting for sales. Then, control your stock effectively. Have sufficient stock to cover your upcoming orders or sales and don't use all your cash in stocks. When you have enough stock and supplies to fill regular orders or maintain expected sales forecasts, have some contingency stock to fill an unexpected and larger orders so that you don't lose customers because you can't deliver on time.

On the other hand, you don't need to go crazy with your stock by overstocking. It's all about planning, understanding your business and the industry you're in, high and low seasons of sales and use your management skills.

"Most people don't plan to fail. They fail to plan - John L. Beckley"

As a business owner, you need to plan your finance as part of your business process. Love it or hate it - just do it and you'll get used to it. It helps you to choose the best way to manage your finance to enable you to reach your goals. If you're not sure where to start, as long as you're doing everything that I've mentioned above, you're already many steps ahead. Looking into details of your daily finance, knowing your numbers and managing your expenses are going to help you see what's happening with your money. When you know what's happening with your money, you'll know exactly what to do with your money and it's always good to ask advice from experts.

To have a bookkeeper, accountant or financial advisor is always a wise thing to do. If you don't know what's happening to your money then they won't be able to help you out as effectively as they can. When they have to find out your money situation to give you useful advice, that's going to cost you more money, as they have to do more work. You're the business owner, take the seat of the boss and tell them what's happening with your money, what future results you're expecting and they'll be able to come up with options for you. Don't give away your power. Use it and be in control.

Living in a moment when it comes to money is not a wise thing to do. What I'm advising is "SAVE". You need to save to make your financial dreams come true. The more money you have the more meaningful things you can do with your life and for others. When you have enough savings and if you're unsure where to invest or to expand your business, hire a financial planner and look into generating more income streams. Savings means having more options in life and business.

Another step that you have to add in to your planning process is budgeting.

"A budget is telling your money where to go instead of wondering where it went - Dave Ramsey"

Budgeting is part of the planning process

Having a budget will allow you to make sure that you're spending less than what you're making and it's the planning for both short and long-term goals. Having a budget doesn't prevent you from having the things you want. Budgeting is something that we all need to have both for our personal and business finances. From the business point of view, it's part of your financial planning process and sticking to your budget is a control tool for your money.

If you want to be financially successful then you have to have a budget. Budgeting is going to make your life easier and also help you to make conscious decisions about how you'll allocate your money. It's a supporting tool towards your retirement plan, emergency plan, a new car or expanding your business.

When you have a solid budget plan in place and know exactly what's happening with your money, you won't have the problem of waking up middle of the night and worrying about money.

Plan your short-term expenses first. So what are your short-term expenses; rent/mortgages, bills, utilities, food, transport, etc.? Don't feel bad to add in whatever you're spending on a monthly basis.

What's in your budgeted monthly income? From your monthly budget, you can see how much you can save if you stick to your budget. I have created a spreadsheet for you. All you need to do it write down your numbers and add them up. By doing this exercise, it's going to tell you how much money you expect to make over the next few months (or years), how much of that money goes out every month and how much you have left to save each month.

If you want to save for your major goals, you have to be careful with your minor spending unless you have a solid plan to generate more income. At the end of the day, it comes down to you. How badly you want to achieve your goals and how far you're willing to go to make your goals come true? Knowing your

numbers will help you take steps to improve your
situation, whether that means focusing on paying off
credit cards to increase your monthly cash flow, or
generating more income from your business so you
can make enough money to afford everything you
need and want.

Then you can start planning for your mid-term
expenses like holidays and long-term expenses like
buying houses and saving for retirement plans. A
budget is your tool to achieve your financial goals.

Don't forget to do a separate budget for your
business because it's monthly expenses too. The same
principle applies to your business finances. It'll help
you manage your expenses more effectively, manage
your cash flow better and support your business plans
in the long term.

Stick to your budget once you have made one. If you
don't stick to your budget, it becomes absolutely
meaningless. For you to stick to your budget, you
need to know your actual financial situation, be
honest with yourself and be realistic while you
prepare your budget.

When you're paying attention to your daily finances
and being in control of them, you have already know
your actual financial situation. You can come up with
budget figures that reflect your actual situation.

"A good money plan is dynamic and changes as your life does. Do a review of your budget each month and make adjustments - Dave Ramsey"

If you don't compare your actual figures to the budgeted figures on a monthly basis, you won't know how well or poorly your business is performing. Why on a monthly basis? Immediate actions are very important in your business when it's required. Reviewing monthly will also allow you to see where you performed well or poorly. You can adjust them as you go before it gets too late and spirals out of control.

Sidenote: This tax section is relevant only within Australia.

Tax is not everyone's a cup of tea

If you ask me, I don't like tax either. But being a business owner, you need to have some knowledge about tax. Having reasonable knowledge about tax will allow you to do the right things. It might motivate you to keep your receipts properly for deductions. You'll know the DOs and DON'Ts and that's going to keep you out of trouble.

If you're a sole trader, the income that you've received from selling your goods and services don't belong to you 100%. You need to pay income tax to the Australian Taxation Office (ATO), so you should keep a portion of it and put it in savings depending on how much income you make. There is a tax table on the ATO website if you wish to know your tax payable. Or you can ask your tax accountant.

When you lodge your tax return, you don't have to freak out that you don't have enough cash to pay tax. If you don't lodge your tax on time and if you have tax payable to ATO, you'll have to pay penalties and interest on the tax payable. I believe you don't want to do that so plan it and get organised.

If you're making AUD $75,000 or more per annum, you need to register for GST. As a sole trader you might take out your clients for coffee. Can you claim it back for tax deduction? Unfortunately, you can't.

Generally, organisations such as companies are allowed to claim most expenses for vehicles that are leased or owned. For sole traders, ATO allows to claim a percentage of motor vehicle expenses based on business use. A log-book may be required for business use and expenses you can claim include petrol, rego, maintenance and insurance.

Your landline, mobile, Internet, fax and Skype are claimable expenses for tax deduction. However if you're using them for both personal and business, you're only entitled to claim the portion used for business.

How can you work out the portion of business use?

Keep a log for 4 weeks and work out a percentage of business usage. That percentage can apply for the whole year.

If you have a home office, your telephone, gas, electricity, cleaning (only business use); office furniture, computer expenses (hardware/software) could be tax deductable. You may also be able to claim a portion of the interest paid on your home loan if you have a dedicated space for your home office. Speak to your tax accountant because when you sell of your house, capital gain tax may be involved.

Business travel expenses are claimable such as air tickets, transportation cost, and accommodation and meal allowances. If you're doing a course or a training that's directly attributable to your work or business, they are claimable as well. Tax is a very board area and as long as you know what expenses are claimable and what aren't, that's a good place to start. Remember, you need to reserve a portion of your profits for tax.

This chapter is about to end and I would like to share a few more things that I personally believe and practice. Try your best every day and the best will come to you. Progression is what you should be looking for, not perfection. Don't give up without trying 100%. Love is powerful so love yourself and love others. Be kind because we are all the same.

We are all travellers, we came to this earth alone and
when we leave the earth we will leave alone.
However, we are here for a reason. The reason is
while we are traveling in this space, for us to find a
purpose in life, live meaningfully and get connected.
So what is your purpose? Find it, live it, learn from it
and share it with the world.

$ Chapter 5

Marketing

"Go the extra mile. It's never crowded."

Whenever I run workshops locally in Perth, Western Australia, online seminars (webinars/teleseminars) or work with my private coaching clients, there's a pattern that I see repeatedly. Many want to jump straight to marketing without having any solid plan.

A sound marketing plan is your roadmap to success.

Yes there are many ways to market your products and services. I'll be covering most of the things here but the thing is, marketing is also about being creative.

Recently I shared in one of my newsletters about advertising and that we're actually artists. If you're not on my weekly newsletters yet, go to www.arabelleyee.com and sign up because I share bits and pieces of information that you can take away and implement straightaway weekly.

We're artists

Artists are creatives. Whether we're offering products or services, when we're creative about what we offer and how we offer then we stand out in the market place.

There are thousands of ads both online and offline.
When you go to Google and do a search, you see lots
of little ads on the right. When you read blogs, you
see lots of ads within the blogs and on the side of the
blogs. When you go onto Facebook, you see
sponsored posts, which are ads. When you go outside,
you see sign-boards, ads on buses, walls and on
benches.

So how do we stand out?

Here are the most important things when you're
marketing.

1. Words

The words we use have a lot of power in persuading
our target audience. I say 'persuading' because I know
a lot of people who 'manipulate' buyers by making
them feel guilty. E.g. If you don't buy my product,
you'll be fat and lonely.

> *"Words can inspire. Words can destroy.
> Choose yours well. – Robin Sharma"*

I said persuade because our buyers are busy in their
daily lives. They're wrapped up in their own worlds
and problems. Sometimes they don't see or seek a
solution. Sometimes, they don't even know there's a
solution. For example, most people don't know they
need a coach. As a Business (and a Transformational)

Coach, sometimes they come to me and say, "I need a marketing plan. Can you create that for me?". No honey, business isn't just about marketing. Business is about understanding ourselves and our target audience so deeply that we can connect to them with ease and confidence.

Words are so important.

When we worked on your target audience earlier in the chapters, we had to define who they are, what are their deepest and darkest fears, dreams and desires. By doing that exercise, we know exactly who we're talking to.

So when we know who our target audience is, then we can use the language that they use. If you've studied NLP (Neuro-linguistic Programming), you'll understand more about the importance of matching and mirroring. It's not just about body language, it's also about using 'their language' so they feel you understand them and they also hear your message.

So this is how you find out the words your target audience use.

Talk to them – Yes. So simple yet not many people are doing. Talk to them directly whether in person, at networking events or online in Facebook Groups or even your business Facebook Page.

Do a survey – Create a set of questionnaires to find

out more about them. Do multiple choice questions because it's easier for them but also let them explain their situation so you can learn their choice of words.

Amazon – Ha! This is the trick not many people in the industry knows! Yes Amazon! It's *the* Gold Mine. If your target market is foodies, then they'll read recipe books or books written by chefs. If your target audience is people with weight issues, they'll read weight loss books or even alternative method books. If your target audience is people looking for love, they'll read dating books.

What you can then do is, read the reviews. Reviews are real words written by real people with real problems. They'll say exactly what you need to hear – why they like the book, what they like the book about and why they don't like it! Note those words!

2. Images

You've heard of "a picture is worth a thousand words", yet many people underestimate the power of the message an image can send. When I do workshops or talks, I very rarely use PowerPoint. If I have to, then I use images.

I do the same thing for my ads. I use Facebook for advertising because my target audience is on Facebook. And when I run Facebook Ads, I pay special attention to what kind of images I use.

Now it comes back to your target audience. You have to choose the image that talks to them while staying aligned to who you're. Someone I know, Kimra Luna, she's a punk rock chick. She has blue hair. She made nearly a million dollar in her first year of her business. She stands out. Every image she uses has her style while choosing them carefully so the images she use speak to her audience.

Sidenote: Please do not ever use Google images. They aren't there for use by others, especially for your website and advertising. However, if you do have to use, please always give credit to the website you got it from. It's ethical and it shows respect. If not, you can get hefty fines.

3. Emotions

Ah! My favourite!

Did you know that when we buy something, we make a decision emotionally and justify it logically?

When people buy that $3,000 handbag, what do they say? "I don't have any bags and I really need this one". They don't need it. They *want* it. But they justify whey they need it – they have a function to go to, $3,000 bag last longer, they're of quality, etc., right?

So now, this isn't about manipulating. This is about connecting to their emotions. If you don't connect them emotionally, they're going to justify it logically which means, no sale.

How do you do that? Again, coming back to knowing your target audience well. What will evoke their emotions? When people are battling with weight issues because they're eating too much, consciously they'll say they just love food. However, deep down there's an underlying problem. It may be that they're unhappy in their lives that they need some comfort. It may be that, food brings memories of having happy family time they once had. Or that she was assaulted when she was young so now her way of protecting herself is to put on weight so she feels secure in her own body. Now these are the real case stories.

So when you advertise your products or services, it's not about 'Hey eat our food, it's so good'. Look at McDonald's ads "So many choices, so little calories". This is targeted to those who want junk food but still don't want to feel guilty about it.

One of the vegan food ads say "Love your mom? So does he" with a picture of a baby cow.

They're speaking to people's emotions.

4. Problems and Solutions

Whatever you're offering, it's somehow solving the problems that people are having. You might not see it that way but it's true. Here are some examples;

- Lighter – So you don't have to make fire with two stones.
- Whiteboard marker – So you don't have to use dirty chalks.
- Tea Sets – So you can have luxury at home with your girl friends.
- Beautiful candles – So you can spice up your love life.

You get the idea. Now think about what kind of problems are your products or services going to solve and talk to their problems.

Website

Did you notice that I'm talking about website only now?

The reason is, if you ask 10 people how they're starting a business, 10 of them will say they're creating a website. Some of them will even pay $5,000 to a web developer to create one for you only to find out they'll have to change a lot. Yes you do need to invest in a beautiful website that show cases your brand and values, however, when you're starting out you need to be mindful of where you spend your money.

With my private coaching clients, I tell them not to worry about their website at first because your website is about telling your story and telling people how you can solve their problems. Remember the words we talked about earlier? Those are the words you'll use on your website. So only when you've done the previous steps and when you've got enough information, then you start creating your website.

Don't make the mistakes that other people do, where they talk about themselves over and over that people never come back to their website. Yes your website is about you but in relations to how you can solve your target audience's problem.

When you're starting out, don't worry about having too many menus or pages on your website. Here are the main ones you need to have, when starting out.

1. Home Page

You only have a few seconds to capture someone's attention. Like I said, people are very busy. When they go to a website, they scan it through <u>very</u> quickly and if they don't like it, they leave. That's it. So on your home page, put up the most important information such as what this website is about, how you can solve their problem, testimonials and link to your Services or Work With Me page.

2. About

This page isn't about your life history. You can definitely write if it's relevant to the work you do but share your story here – how you got started, what's your why and what they can get by working with you.

3. Services or Work With Me

Now this is about your offerings – program, packages or products you're selling. Your website need to generate income for you, meaning if you have low cost items that people can buy, don't make them leave your website. Make them buy straight away by putting 'Buy Now' buttons.

4. Contact

Clearly, you want people to contact you so include your email, phone or address whatever is relevant to your business. I also suggest you to have a contact form that people can fill to enquire about your services as well.

Social Media

We all know that Social Media is the way to go right now. Even if you have an offline business, having a social media presence helps boost your business. Look at even large corporations, they're now coming onto social media because it allows them to connect with their target audience and they're hiring teams to manage their social media so they can respond to individual requests and comments timely. The reason why they're doing this is because it helps them build that trust and relationship with their customers.

As small business owners, this is a tool that can help
you generate millions of dollars. I personally know
millionaires who generate millions of dollars from
social media.

The question is, how do you harness the power of
Social Media?

First thing first, there are many social media platforms
that you can use – Twitter, Facebook, LinkedIn,
Instagram, Tumblr, Periscope, Blab, etc. at the time
of writing this book.

Which one would you use?

Again it comes back to your target audience. Where
are they? Where do they hang out? And what are you
offering? E.g. If you have product-based business,
Instagram could potentially be the platform for you
because Instagram is about using images. So when
you do your target audience research, these are the
things you'll need to find out so you can choose the
right platform.

A private coaching client of mine came to me and
said she's been using Facebook for her business but
she wasn't getting anywhere. So we worked through
identifying where her target market was and we found
out they are on LinkedIn.

That's why it's important for you to find out where

your target market is before you invest your time and money in social media or anything of that matter.

The second question is how do we use social media? Social media can definitely help you generate income but there's a strategy behind it. People are already on social media everyday for 'social' reasons so you can't push your products and services to them. You have to build a relationship and speak to them in a way that will make them want to connect with you. It's the 80/20 rule where 80% of the time you share things that are useful for them; quotes, interesting articles, your own blog posts, images, fun things and you promote the 20%.

Now the reason why you want to have social media is because you want to have raving fans or a great following. Growing your social media presence will also boost your credibility. By sharing quality content that are fun, engaging, interesting and educational, your following will grow over time. You can also run advertisements on social media to grow your following as well e.g. Facebook Ads.

How do you then convert your following into paying customers? You move them into your database by offering free opt-ins (we'll talk more about this in a bit) and you can start selling. So it works like this:

Now the question I get asked a lot is what can I post?
Before we go into what you can post, we need to
think of *why* you're posting.

Start with an end goal in mind.

What do you want to achieve from your social media
– raving fans, personal branding, educate people,
build trust or share love? Your content needs to be
planned depending on the outcome you want.

With that end goal in mind, I'm going to give you a
few ideas of what you can post with inspiration from
Boom Social.

1.   State a problem and ask for advice. E.g. I'm
writing a new book and I need help choosing a title.

2.   Run a poll. E.g. I'm running a workshop next
month and I'd like to know which topic you'd be
most interested in.

3.   Inspirational quotes. People just love them!

4.   Fill in the blank. E.g. I'm_____today

5.   Blog posts. When you write blogs, share them on
social media to drive traffic and to position yourself
as the expert.

6.   Cross promote. If someone you know has a great
offer, share it on your social media so your tribe feels

that you're all about giving value and the other person also will want to help you out in return.

7.   Tips. E.g. How to _____.

8.   Behind the scene. Share your personal posts, what you're doing today, what your office looks like or even the picture of your family. But only once in a while.

9.   Be vulnerable. Share what you're struggling with. It makes you human.

10.   Testimonials or case studies. Share about the success your customers are having after working with you.

11.   Videos. A great way for people to see who's behind the brand, build like, trust and credibility.

12.   Share other blog posts. If you find something interesting and relevant, share it with your tribe.

13.   Q&A Day. Set a day aside and let them ask you questions so you can solve their problems publicity. What a great way to share your expertise!

Collaborations

Since the very early days of my business, I realised the potential of collaborations. I don't believe in competitions.

*"Go alone if you want to go fast. Go with
others if you want to go further."*

So I built my network, gave a ton of value to people
and I've had help from friends, peers, complimentary
businesses and even Thought Leaders and
Millionaires to share my message and expand my
reach to many people.

So how do you identify who would be a good fit to
collaborate with? This is a strategic move. After all,
we're doing business here.

Here are a few things you need to note;

1. Values

The person or the company you collaborate has to
share the same values towards life, business and
customers as you.

2. Complimentary Businesses

When you collaborate with another business, it's
better to collaborate with a business that's
complimentary to yours. The reason is if it's the same
type of business, you could potentially be competing
with each other rather than support one another. So
what are the complimentary businesses?

For example, if you're a Health Coach, you can

collaborate with a Fitness Trainer. Remember how you have ATMs in the gas stations? It's a collaboration of some sort. There are so many ways you can collaborate. You can do referrals where you pay a certain percentage to the other business who refers you. You can also create joint promotions where you split the profits. You can run workshops together or even advertise for each other. Ways to collaborate with complimentary businesses are limitless.

As long as you're creative, you can have a collaboration. If you want to learn more about collaborations, you can download my free resource here.

3. Affiliate Marketing

This is about creating affiliates who will sell your products or services for you. Here are some examples of affiliate marketing – Amazon: when you set up as an affiliate, you get an affiliate account through which you can get your own links to the books you like. You can then sell those books and if people buy through your link, you get commission. The same applies for your business as well. If you have a book, a program or a course that you want others to sell for you, you need to create an affiliate link that they can use so when people sign up through their links, they get commission. How much commission you pay out has to be agreed up front. This is one way that can be extremely lucrative if you do it right.

4. Written agreements

When you collaborate with someone, it's important to
have everything agreed and written.

Blogs

You hear about writing blogs all the time. It's one of
the most lucrative ways of generating passive or even
direct income. You can monetise your blog. However,
there's a strategy behind it.

Ramit Sethi from www.IWillTeachYouToBeRich.com
once mentioned about a lady who wrote 200 blogs
but never really generated any income from her blog.
That's because there was no strategy.

So let's first talk about why writing a blog is a
strategic move.

Anyone can write a blog but what you write is
important. It's always about *content* and *context*
meaning what you write needs to be relevant, has
value and a strategy. Again, it's about starting with the
end goal in mind. What would you like to achieve
from your blog? Do you want more clients? Do you
want to sell something? Do you want to advertise
your new product? Do you want to build your email
database?

I've been fortunate enough to be featured in the major online publications writing about business and mindset. As a result, I'm able to share my message, expand my reach and sell my programs. One of the programs that's popular is called Unconventional Expert. It's about helping startup soloprenuer get a clear strategy so that they can build a successful business. With one blog post I generated $970 on the first day. More over, blog posts get shared and can be read anytime which means this product has become 'evergreen' or passive income for me. It sells by itself.

So when you write a blog post, think about the end goal you want to achieve and put a specific Call To Action at the end. It looks something like this –

- Blog post about (your topic)

- Before it ends, use a segue.

- Would you like to learn more about how to (solve the problem)? Click here to (schedule a free session with me and put a link to it.)

That's one strategy of writing *your own* blog post.

What about writing for major publications?

When you're starting out, you don't have a lot of following. It's very hard for people to beat a path down to your door. Therefore, it's easier if you can write for blog sites with a big following so you can

have more exposure and build credibility. So think
about popular blog sites in your industry.

How do you pitch them?

Once you have identified the popular blog sites you
want to write for, you need to learn their tone, style
and their audience. Is that the audience you're
targeting? If yes, you can contact the editor directly,
through the contact form or some sites have
Contribute To Us section. That's where you can pitch
why you should write for them with a sample of your
blog post.

Once you got in, that's it! Write something that has
content and *context*, and you're on your way to
becoming an authority in your field!

Email Marketing

When you think about email marketing, what comes
to your mind? It's the similar concept as when you do
online shopping, you sign up or you have to provide
your email address before you check out and then you
receive weekly newsletters. However, depending on
the nature of your business, what you send out in the
newsletters will be different from business to
business.

Why do we want to do this? Email marketing helps us
create a relationship with our potential customers.
Once you've built that relationship and trust, it makes

it easier for you to sell and for them to buy.

Whether you're a coach, author, speaker or even a product based business, this is something you should do on an ongoing basis. If you speak to many business leaders, they'll tell you that *your money is in your list*. That list is the email database. The bigger your database is the more you'll be able to sell.

So how do you build the list? There are a couple of ways of doing that.

1. Free giveaway

When you go to a cosmetic counter to find a moisturiser, you get to use a tester to see if the product is what you're looking for. When you like it, you might buy a small bottle to so you can try it first. This is the low entry product. It's risk-free for them and you can also showcase what they'll get when they buy a bigger bottle.

The same concept applies to your business. Whether you have a product or service-based business, you can giveaway something for free.

For example, many people giveaway their books. If you're a coach or consultant, you can give away a checklist, report, free audio program or video series. This is endless. There are cafes who let people try small bite size of their cakes. Starbucks usually give out small sample cups of their coffee.

2. Sale

When someone buys your product, you can
automatically collect their email address when they
give permission to receive weekly newsletter.

3. Running joint webinars or seminars

This is a collaboration you do with someone else.
When the person you collaborate with has a big
following and when you both have an agreement in
place, you can also collect emails through
registrations.

The reason why you need to build your list is because
your target audience out there. They don't know you
and they have never interacted with you, yet. They are
called *cold leads*, meaning you haven't built that like,
trust and credibility yet.

So by them joining your email list and by you sending
out weekly, bi-weekly or monthly newsletter, you're
taking them along the journey so that they can get to
know you more. They then become *warm leads*. Once
they know you, it's easier for you to start selling
through email. The typical percentage is 2-3% of your
list that buys your products.

I know you're already thinking of "What am I
supposed to email them weekly?". That's what I'm
going to tell you next. Depending on the type of

business you have, what you email out will be different. For example, Tax Accountants can send out regular tax updates or tax tips, Hair Dressers can send out the hair styles or even the well-known customers they have, a Coach or Consultant can send out how-to emails or tips and if you sell Chocolates, you can send out pictures of your amazing chocolates or even behind the scenes of how you make those chocolates!

You can build your list through many ways.

4. Website

Create a free opt-in on your website so people can sign up when they land on your site e.g. Recipes, How To PDF, Tips, Report, etc.

5. Social Media

Share the page of your free opt-in so people can sign up.

6. Contest

People love to be part of contests and to be part of the contest, they have to sign up.

7. Challenges

30 Days Fitness Challenge, 21 Days Quit Smoking Challenge, 7 Days Business Challenge – these are all popular challenges that people like to be part of.

Again, this comes back to content planning. The key
here is to plan out your content plan a month ahead
so you know exactly what you're sending each week
or whatever frequency that applies to your business.

Here's a quick tip to plan your content: start with
titles of what you want to talk about and then expand
them into short posts for your newsletters.

Marketing Plan

Now is the time for you to start creating your
marketing plan. I suggest that you start with 2-weeks
marketing plan so you don't overwhelm yourself.
From there, you should progress to a 30-day
marketing plan.

Here I'm combine content plan and marketing plan
for you so it's easy for you to manage. As you grow,
you can make this more advanced. I believe in less is
more so let's start with this one.

*Tips: Start with end goal in mind. What do you want to
achieve within the next 30 days?*

Simple Marketing Plan

Date	Task	FB Page	FB Group 1	FB Group 2	*Newsletters*	*Others*
1 Jun	Post	Blog	Question	-	Tips	Create free opt-in
2 Jun						

* FB – Facebook

$ Chapter 6

Sales

What a journey we've come all the way! Now let's talk about sales, shall we? Before I go on further, let's start with a quick exercise.

What you hear the word 'sales', what comes to your mind? Write down as many words as you can.

Negative	Positive

It's important that you do this exercise before you go on further because sales is all about your beliefs and your opinions about it.

Many people I've worked with are scared of sales. That's because of our past experiences with salesy sales people who pushed and manipulated us to buy things that we didn't need. Whenever I do this exercise with my private clients, these are the words that come up quite regularly; icky, pushy, disgusting, manipulative, horrible and greedy. Of course when we go out and sell with that belief, the people who we're selling our products or services to will feel the same way towards us.

So what exactly is sales?

When I sell, *I'm helping people buy back their time so they can do things that matter.* See, one thing that I tell people is that, if you need money for rent, please don't ever sell because you're going to be desperate to make that money. If you need money, find a job first and support your business financially.

Now you know money is energy. Everything we do is energy. Every word, every action and every communication between two people is all about energy.

So before we learn how to sell, the first thing we need to do is a mindset shift about sales.

Mindset

When I run workshops, I ask people "who's the sales person here?" and I see only a few hands coming up.

Did you know that we're all sales people? Whatever
we're telling people about us, whatever we're posting
on social media or even when we're talking to friends,
we're selling something – an idea about who we are
and an idea about what we want them to do.

Sales people are very important because without sales
people, which are all of us, the world will come to a
stop. In our society, we're all buying something
everyday and that's the driver that's creating the
momentum in our society.

Selling is about mindset. What goes on in your mind
is what makes you succeed or not succeed. Tim Ferris
had once done a challenge with University students
where he asked them to contact the 'seemingly
impossible to contact' celebrities and ask them 3
questions, and whoever wins get the all paid round-
trip ticket anywhere in the world. Of course majority
of them straightaway said before even trying how
difficult and impossible the task was. However, was it
impossible? No, because some of the students were
able to do that. Were they particularly smarter? No, it
was just all about mindset.

When you sell with confidence, conviction, love and
belief in your product or services, it'll be conveyed in
your both verbal and non-verbal message. That's what
people buy.

Another thing is the income you make from your

sales is directly proportional to the income ceiling you've created for yourself. Of course you need to be realistic as well. If you're starting and if you're aiming 1 million dollar in the first three months, you're probably a little over ambitious. Set realistic income goals that you can achieve every quarter or so and expand your comfort zone from there.

Sales is 80/20 rules

20% of your efforts should create 80% of results for you. What does that mean?

It means that you need to have everything in the previous chapters in place, all the processes and systems in place so that when you've created a system of how you're going to sell, it should all sell automatically for you.

For example, if you're a Real Estate Agent, rather that sitting at your desk calling people all day (which would be putting 80% effort), you choose a time and day that people will be most accessible – say in the mornings – then you make all your calls in the morning and move away from your phone and do something else during the day.

I knew someone in the corporate job who runs all his meetings only in the mornings because he knew that people are fresh, they are likely to produce ideas and likely to accept his ideas. People get overwhelmed and stressed out as the day goes by and he always said he

never wanted to be the one who runs meetings in the
evenings. This is being smart. That's the 80/20 rule.
He makes decisions at the start of the day and
whatever comes up during the day is mostly no longer
valid because decisions and progress have been made.

Creativity

You may be selling the same thing as your
competitors but it's all about being creative. I always
ask my clients "How are you different from your
competitors" and that's when most people are stuck.
How you differentiate yourself depends on your
creativity. Have you seen TV commercials that show
a story that connects to human emotions and at the
end they flash a product only for a split second?
Advertising companies know very well how to evoke
emotions in the consumers. You don't need to talk
about the product throughout the commercial.

Look at Pepsi's commercial with Michael Jackson
called "Pepsi Generation". Michael Jackson is the
king of evoking emotions. He dances and he does
what he does. There are a group of kids drinking
Pepsi and dancing his moves. The whole idea of the
commercial is about being cool, fun and happy which
means drinking Pepsi is cool, fun, happy and that
you'll belong to that *Pepsi Generation*. That's the
emotion they're linking to people. You can click here
to watch.

Get inspired

Whichever industry you're in, there's always someone who's doing really well. It's always good to model someone who's successful. Modelling another business isn't copying. It's about getting inspiration and understanding what sets them apart from the rest.

Do a case study of the business; what are they doing right and what are they doing wrong. Learn and create a sales model that will fit yours.

Mastery

Now selling is a skill. It's definitely something you can learn and master over time. What you need is the right mindset, strategy, commitment and repetition.

"Progress begins at the end of your comfort zone"

That's right. You need to push your boundaries to get better at sales. Nothing will happen with you sitting and feeling icky about it. Everyone has to start somewhere and confidence comes from taking action. You have to start before you're ready, otherwise you'll never get started.

1. Set yourself a challenge – If you believe that you're not good at sales and that you're terrible when making calls, set yourself a 7-day challenge where you're to call one person a day and sell. After 7 days,

you'll have spoken to 7 people and your ability to sell
will have improved so much more.

2. Create affirmations – As I said before, the words
you use have massive impact on the psychology of
your target audience and the same is true for your
own psychology as well. "I am" are the two magical
words that we tend to use in the wrong ways such as
"I'm bad at sales" "I'm not good enough" and what
you're doing is you're subconsciously affirming your
belief of what you're not. So why not you turn it
around and start saying, "I'm good at sales", "I'm
wealth", "I'm confident", "I'm money magnet" and
see what happens next.

3. Love yourself – Yes! If you love yourself and love
what you do, people will fall in love with you too.
Have you ever seen someone who's so excited about
what they're selling that you get so excited about
buying it too? People love buying! Full stop! Love
yourself and make them love you for giving them
what they want.

4. Boost your confidence – The best time to boost
your confidence is after making a sale. When you
make your first sale, your confidence will be sky high.
That's the best time for you to go out and make
another sale. That will boost your confidence even
more. So don't start feeling so complacent after your
first sale. Keep doing it and it'll become natural to

you.

5. Guide them through – When people buy, they can be indecisive of what to do next. This is especially true if the product or service is of high price. You're the one who have to guide them through. If you're confused of the next steps, they will be too. One mistake I see in a lot of people is that because of the fear of rejection, they tell people to go home and think. No! You don't do that. When people go home and think, they start thinking of the trip they need to take, the car they need to fix and all the million other things they need do and what you're selling becomes less important. However in reality, it may be the very thing they need right now!

6. Visualise – Visualisation is not a woowoo thing where you just sit and hope. Our brain is wired in a way that when we visualise, we're preparing ourselves for the future scenarios as if they're happening now and we're mentally ready. So visualise yourself getting on the phone or meeting your prospect and selling confidently. It's an exercise you can do for free everyday and you'll be surprised what a difference it can make in reality.

7. Hold yourself accountable – Now here's my favourite part. I suggest you create a calendar of a challenge you'll create for yourself and also how many people you'll talk to, to practise selling. Put a date in the calendar that by this date, you'll have spoken and sold to 'x' number of people. That way, you can hold yourself accountable and make selling easier for you.

Buyer's psychology

Now that you know the psychology that you need to have to be able to make successful sales, let's talk about buyer's psychology.

It takes two to complete a successful sale. The more you understand the psychology of your buyers, the more you'll be able to master this.

When people buy, they make emotional decisions and they justify logically. That's why you need to be able to connect to people's emotions.

1. When people buy, two things happen; loss of money and gain of their purchase. So in order for them to make a decision to buy, you need to increase their buying desire so it outweighs the fear of loss. How do you do that? There are many ways you can do this; you can highlight the benefits they're getting from making this purchase, you can provide guarantees such as 60 days money back guarantee or something similar or a guarantee of seeing the result they desire e.g. lose 5kg in 30 days.

2. When people say they want to think again, that shows that either they don't see in the value in what you're selling or they don't think they really need it right now. That's when you have to do a bit more

work by asking them what is the reason why they think they need to think over. A good sales person knows how to ask the right questions. Ask them what's stopping them from making the decision, what they're expecting or simply what's on their mind.

3. Another thing that's important is to talk to the key decision maker. If it's a couple making the purchase together, find out who makes decisions when it comes to money because once the decision maker has subconsciously made a decision to buy, the other person will follow the decision.

4. When you talk to you potential customer, as a newbie sales person, we tend to speak very fast and we tend to fill in the silences with words. That's a wrong move. Learn to speak slower and create pauses. Pauses let people think, allow you to understand where they are and allow you to gather your thoughts what to say next.

5. In today's market, honesty and authenticity are something people are looking for. We've all had bad experiences with con sales people. If you don't have the feature they want, tell them you don't have it but you're happy to think of something else that they can have. If you don't know something, say the three magic words "*I don't know* but I can find out about that for you". Nothing beats honesty.

6. Your body language plays a big role when you see

potential customers face to face and your tone plays a big role when you talk to them on the phone. Practise selling in front of the mirror and record yourself. Evaluate if you'd buy from yourself.

Now here's the last part of making a sales. Follow these steps when you talk to your potential customers and you'll be sure to make a close.

1. Identify the problem.

2. Make them understand what would happen if they don't solve that problem.

3. Paint the picture what it would be like if they can get the problem solved.

4. Ask open-ended questions and if you don't fully understand what they're explaining, don't be afraid to clarify e.g. What would it be like for you if you can solve this problem today? How would your life transform if you buy this today?

5. Listen rather than talk.

6. Give them a solution to their problem, that is, your products or services.

7. Make it risk-free for them if you can e.g. 60 days money back guarantee.

8. Ask close-ended questions to close the sale e.g. Are

you ready to get started today?

9. Discuss about the price at last (Never leave the conversation with *affordability*. Always end the conversation with *possibility*)

Selling is an art and a skill. That's something you can acquire, improve and master with commitment and repetition. Set a number of people you want to practice selling for the next 30 days until you get comfortable. Role-play with your family and friends.

When you've mastered selling, running a business becomes so much more exciting for you. I wish you all the best and I hope this book has helped you tremendously in your journey of starting a business that you're passionate about.

Love and light,

Arabelle

Join The Tribe

Would you like to be part of a global community of women who are taking actions and creating change in their life, business and in the world?

Here's how you can be part of;

1. Sign up to receive weekly inspiration, tips and free mentoring newsletters to help you with your life and business here at www.arabelleyee.com

2. You can also join us on Facebook.

3. Did you love this book? Or do you have any questions you want answered, email to us at teamarabelle@thecalmedge.com.

Success Stories

"I was lost and in need of guidance. Everything has changed in my life and business. I started to believe in myself again. I even developed a new company in the process. I would recommend everyone that really wants to be on business to work with Arabelle." - Sophie Solmini, Wellness Coach

"I have to say thank you again. Just gone through some of your modules, and I'm already getting a new perspective on my business. You have an excellent way of speaking, encouraging and giving instructions. You provide really applicable values" - Iren Hope Ronhovde

"You gave me insight into defining out what direction and ultimate goal for our business. I have a plan that I'm already implementing for building a client base and more defined services." - Paula Lister - Owner and Consultant at Becoming More Wellness Spa

"Thank you Arabelle for the amazing coaching session! I loved that instead of telling me 'what I wanted to hear' you told me what I needed to hear. Your suggestions were very smart and in a very kind way, you helped me realize that my original action plan wasn't necessarily aligned to my ultimate vision. You gave me great insight and provided the guidance to take the necessary steps. For those of you who are debating booking a session with Arabelle I highly recommend it!" - Marketing Consultant, Vanesa CF

*"Arabelle opened clarity to what I could see no further on. A
treasure to work with and continue to grow with. So full of
passion insight knowledge and love." – Aleigha Cox*

*"Excellent coaching with Arabelle! It was so helpful being able
to talk through my biggest struggles - money! I'm sure lots of
you can relate! She gave me practical ways to make a change
and she was kind and caring in her approach! Thank you
Arabelle!" - Michelle Elman, Body Confidence Coach*

Special Thanks

First of all I'd like to thank Aundria Khine for contributing to the Finance chapter of this book. As a Financial Coach, she helps and supports start up women entrepreneurs to have their money power so that they are not stressed or overwhelmed when it comes to dealing with financial matters. She provides helpful steps to achieve financial goals, which are practical, simple, effective and easy to follow. So if you find the finance chapter useful and if you'd like to connect with her, you can find her at www.nirvanafinance.com or connect with her on Facebook.

Secondly, I'd like to thank Kathryn High. I've been debating in my head which book to start writing; a business book (this one) or a raw, honest and organic truth about mindset, spirituality and personal transformations. But then I believe that the universe has a way of sending the right angels at the right time. We were sitting at a café one day and Kath brought up the topic of writing a business book to help startup female business owners. So as usual, I acted on it and here you're reading this book. Kath is a Clinical Hypnotherapist helping people overcome various psychological barriers blocking them in their lives. If you'd like to find out more about her, you can reach her at www.clarityhypnosis.com.au.

Resources

The following are services and tools that can help you in the process of starting your business.

Free downloads

1. Free Money Block Audio: How to master your money mindset. Learn about;

- The limiting beliefs that are holding you back from creating wealth
- Ways you haven't explored that you can make more money from
- Practical steps to master your mindset

2. Essential Kit For Startup Coaches: 10 simple ways to be more visible, get more clients and make sales.

3. Target Market Identification Workbook: A comprehensive cheat sheet to give you clarity and strategy to get your clients right now.

- The exact steps I use to find my ideal clients.
- 34 ways to know your clients inside out.
- 8 steps to start getting clients straight away

Tools

LeadPages

For Landing Pages or squeeze pages. I used to create

landing/squeeze pages in my website but the painful part was, I had to come up with the design, do everything myself which took a lot of time and couldn't track how many people were visiting. However, with LeadPages, I was able to analyse the analytics. For example, if people are visiting my landing pages and not opting in, it's a sign that I need to tweak the landing page. I could also create A/B tests which means I could split test several landing pages to see which one performs better.

Acuity Scheduling

If you see clients, this is a must for you. Acuity syncs your calendar so your clients can see the real-time. It takes away the pain of you having to schedule everything yourself; automate the administrative side of your business. You can also create buffer so in case your appointment goes over, you still have buffer for the next appointment. Clients can also make payments via PayPal because Acuity can integrate with PayPal. It also integrates with MailChimp which means, all your potential clients booking sessions will be stored directly in MailChimp.

MailChimp

You get the first 500 emails for free. When you starting out, this is free and easy to use. You can collect email and create auto-responders, which are automated email campaigns. You can also schedule

your email campaigns in advance or let MailChimp
schedule them.

<u>Wix</u> - Wix is super easy to use. It's drag and drop. It
doesn't take a long time for you to learn. My website
is created with wix and I did it all myself, so you can
you!

About The Author

Arabelle Yee is a passionate expert at creating transformations for people in life and business through coaching, speaking and living what she teaches herself.

Originally from Burma, Arabelle grew up being taught about traditions, culture and fitting into the rather small society for acceptance. Being ever so driven, thinking outside of the frame and true to herself, Arabelle always questioned "Is there more to life than what we are now?" After she went through major challenges in her life, she found herself creating massive transformations and results in her life; emotionally, spiritually and financially.

Bringing a decade of experience in working with hundreds of people, delivering workshops and creating results into her work, she now works with women from across the globe inspiring and empowering them so they can create extraordinary results in both life and business. As a spiritual person at heart, avid learner of life experiences, Clinical Psychotherapist and NLP Practitioner, she also frequently writes in major publications about mindset, spirituality and business.

Arabelle's mission is to share her message to inspire and empower people and she's open for discussion if you'd like her to speak at your next event. You can

connect with her through her website or connect with
her on social media.

Website: www.arabelleyee.com

Facebook: www.facebook.com/arabelleyeecoaching

Twitter: www.twitter.com/arabelleyee